THE OFFICIAL
VISUAL COMPANION

THE SCARLET SPEEDSTER FROM PAGE TO SCREEN

THE OFFICIAL
VISUAL COMPANION

THE SCARLET SPEEDSTER FROM PAGE TO SCREEN

By Randall Lotowycz

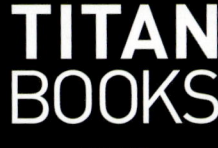

LONDON

Introduction | 07

CHAPTER 1
THE WORLD OF THE FLASH

The Flash's Origin | 10

Building the Cinematic Multiverse | 13

The Flash Suit | 16

Nora Onscreen | 20

Introducing Iris West | 26

Welcome to Central City | 30

Barry's Crime-Fighting Career | 34

CHAPTER 2
SUPER-SPEED

The Flash in Action | 44

The Speed Force | 50

CHAPTER 3
FLASHBACK!

Discovering the Chronobowl | 56

Flashpoint | 62

A Tale of Two Barrys | 64

CHAPTER 4
HEROES AND VILLAINS

The Dark Knight Returns | 72

A World Without Superman | 82

Young Flash, Old Suit | 88

Dark Flash | 94

INTRODUCTION

"THIS IS THE STARTLING TALE OF THE FLASH—A MAN SO FAST THAT HE NOT ONLY OUTRACED HIS SHADOW—BUT ALSO BROKE THROUGH THE SOUND BARRIER—ON FOOT!"

So began the very first Barry Allen story within the pages of *DC's Showcase* #4 in October 1956. The story detailed the freak accident involving a bolt of lightning and some laboratory chemicals that gave the police scientist his incredible speed powers, which he used as The Flash. Nothing was ever the same since that fateful accident, and Barry Allen never stopped running.

Over the past seventy-plus years, The Flash has been an essential part of the DC Multiverse. In fact, as you'll learn, he was the first Super Hero to discover the Multiverse and cross over to a parallel universe with a Flash of its own. His adventures have extended beyond the page to multiple television series, each putting their own spin on the mythos.

Now, with the release of *The Flash*, Barry Allen finally has his own film—a cinematic adventure to behold. Never before have Barry's powers been explored and realized as they are now on the big screen. Try to keep up as we do a marathon run through the film's making, profiling all the key characters and the ways in which filmmaker Andy Muschietti realizes the most fantastical elements of The Flash's story. We'll also look back at Barry's comic book history and previous live-action incarnations to reveal everything that makes him the fastest man alive.

CHAPTER 1

THE WORLD OF THE FLASH

THE FLASH'S ORIGIN

Welcome to the whirlwind adventures of the Fastest Man Alive! After guest appearances in recent DC films and TV shows, The Flash is ready for the spotlight with his own film.

WHEN LIGHTNING STRIKES

As a freshman in college, Barry Allen (played by Ezra Miller) interned at the Central City Crime Lab, committed to becoming a crime scene investigator and proving his father did not murder his mother when Barry was eight years old. On the night of September 29, as a thunderstorm raged outside, Barry worked late into the night. Shortly after opening a window to air out the laboratory from fumes, he took a seat below a shelf of chemicals. In an instant, a bolt of lightning blazed through the window, striking the chemicals. The vials exploded, raining electrified liquid down upon Barry. It should have killed him. But as his skin hissed and burned, something miraculous happened: Barry rapidly began to heal. Soon, he discovered healing wasn't the only thing that had accelerated. He could now move at super-speeds far greater than humanly possible.

THE FLASH TODAY!

As the movie *The Flash* begins, Barry is a few years older and slightly more experienced as a Super Hero than he was in *Justice League*. But, as Ezra Miller comments, "[Barry's] still desperately trying to rectify and reconcile the traumas of his life," meaning his mother's murder and his father's incarceration.

THE BIG LEAGUES

Determined to do good with his abilities, Barry started small and ran under the radar. One day he returned to his base of operations to find Bruce Wayne (played by Ben Affleck) waiting for him. The Caped Crusader was building a team of metahumans and wanted Barry to join him. Despite being relatively inexperienced and unsure of himself in combat, Barry immediately agreed, and his abilities came in handy as a member of the Justice League.

THE FIRST SPEEDSTER

Jay Garrick was the first iteration of The Flash. His chest adorned with a lightning bolt, he was able to run at supersonic speeds. Created by writer Gardner Fox and artist Harry Lampert, the World War II–era hero was first introduced in *Flash Comics* #1 (January 1940). Unlike Barry, Jay didn't wear a mask. Instead, he was known for his signature winged helmet, inspired by Mercury, the Roman god known for his great speed. He served alongside the Justice Society of America and acted as a mentor to other speedsters in his later years.

BARRY ALLEN HAS ENTERED THE RACE

When Barry Allen debuted in *Showcase* #4 (October 1956), he was an established forensic scientist for the Central City Police Department and he was renowned for two things—being late and solving cases that flummoxed his colleagues. As in the film, Barry's fateful accident takes place one night and he decides to call himself The Flash. Unlike the film, later retellings of Barry's origin story reveal that he spent four months in a coma before awaking to discover his speed powers.

BUILDING THE CINEMATIC MULTIVERSE

Though the concept is well established in the comics, the actions of Barry Allen in The Flash *introduce the Multiverse to the big screen for the first time—where changing the past is retrocausal, changing the future* and *the past; timelines run almost parallel with one another, with moments of intersection and divergence. Producer Barbara Muschietti was particularly excited to bring this concept to life with The Flash. She shares that the film ushers in "a new frontier [from which] many stories can exist." Using The Flash's first solo film to introduce the Multiverse aligns perfectly with Barry Allen's own comic debut.*

THE FLASH AND THE MULTIVERSE

The very concept of the DC Multiverse began with Barry's first appearance in *Showcase* #4. This issue heralded the start of the Silver Age of comics. DC decided to introduce fresh incarnations of some of their characters for a new generation. This included The Flash, with Barry replacing Jay Garrick, whose time in the spotlight had ended several years before Barry made his debut.

Writer Robert Kanigher and artists Carmine Infantino and Joe Kubert paid tribute to Jay Garrick (who had not appeared in a comic for five years) within the pages of *Showcase* #4 by having Barry read the very same Golden Age *Flash Comics* that real-life comic readers enjoyed. After receiving his speed powers, Barry even decided to name himself after Jay. This small moment of one comic book character reading about another comic character planted the seeds of the Multiverse that would continue to grow throughout the pages of *The Flash*.

In September 1961's *The Flash* #123, titled "The Flash of Two Worlds," Barry discovered that Jay Garrick was more than just a comic book character when he accidentally transported himself to a parallel Earth in which Jay lived. This encounter was the first of many between them. Barry's reality was dubbed Earth–

One within the pages of *Justice League of America*; Jay's was designated Earth-Two. Over a nearly twenty-five-year period, many crossovers ensued—between not only these two Earths but also *hundreds* of others, each designated by numbers and letters. But as DC neared its fiftieth anniversary, the Multiverse felt unwieldy and a changeup was in order.

The 1985 *Crisis on Infinite Earths* limited series, written by Marv Wolfman and illustrated by George Pérez, spelled the end of the Multiverse. Nothing would be the same once the cosmic threat known as the Anti-Monitor destroyed Earth after Earth in the Multiverse. Super Heroes of the remaining Earths banded together to stop the Anti-Monitor, which they did at great cost. Multiple Super Heroes died, including Barry Allen. In the wake of the Anti-Monitor's defeat, only a single universe remained. If the Multiverse's existence was intrinsically tied to Barry Allen's creation, it was sadly fitting to see its end marked by his death. Though he was gone, Barry's heroics inspired new generations of speedsters, starting with his sidekick Wally West taking on the mantle of The Flash.

Throughout the comics, subsequent crises struck over the years, each with startling results. One saw the rebirth of the Multiverse. Another saw Barry brought back to life. After the events of the 2020 *Dark Nights: Death Metal* miniseries by writer Scott Snyder and artist Greg Capullo, the Multiverse was created anew with infinite worlds and possibilities. Ever curious, Barry joined the Justice League Incarnate, an assembly of Super Heroes from throughout the Multiverse, and was tasked with exploring and mapping all the newly created Earths. With his abilities and intellect, Barry was practically born for the assignment.

ACROSS THE MULTIVERSE

In both the 1990 and the 2014 *The Flash* television series, starring John Wesley Shipp and Grant Gustin, respectively, the circumstances of when and why Barry Allen was in the crime lab that fateful night may have changed, but that bolt of lightning and the nearby chemicals were constants, cementing Barry's fate as The Flash.

THE FLASH SUIT

Normal fabrics don't stand a chance when Barry starts running, with friction at high speeds causing his clothes to disintegrate. Something stronger is required.

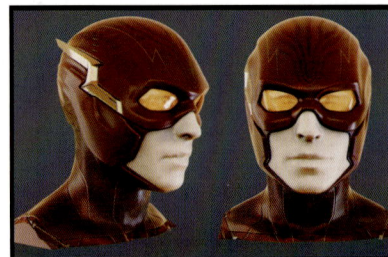
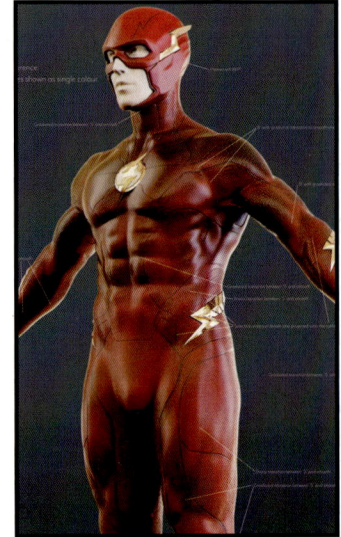

THE EVOLUTION OF THE FLASH'S LOOK

In the movie *The Flash*, we get a glimpse of Barry's previously unseen past, when he travels to Metropolis to provide aid during Zod's attack—the very same events depicted in the film *Man of Steel*, although The Flash is not seen in that film. The Flash wore an extremely makeshift suit during Zod's attack. Though it provides some protection via a bike helmet and sports pads, it is held together by duct tape and not meant for long-term use.

By the time Batman recruits Barry in 2017's *Justice League*, the speedster has fashioned a sturdier suit. Made from the same silica-based sand quartz material used to protect space shuttles from burning up on reentry, the suit is abrasion- and heat-resistant, enabling it to withstand Barry's high velocities.

With Batman's help, Barry designs an update of his suit. It's made from a chemically compressed synthetic silk with a bonded outer layer of ultrasmooth Teflon, allowing for high-speed travel while remaining thermally stable.

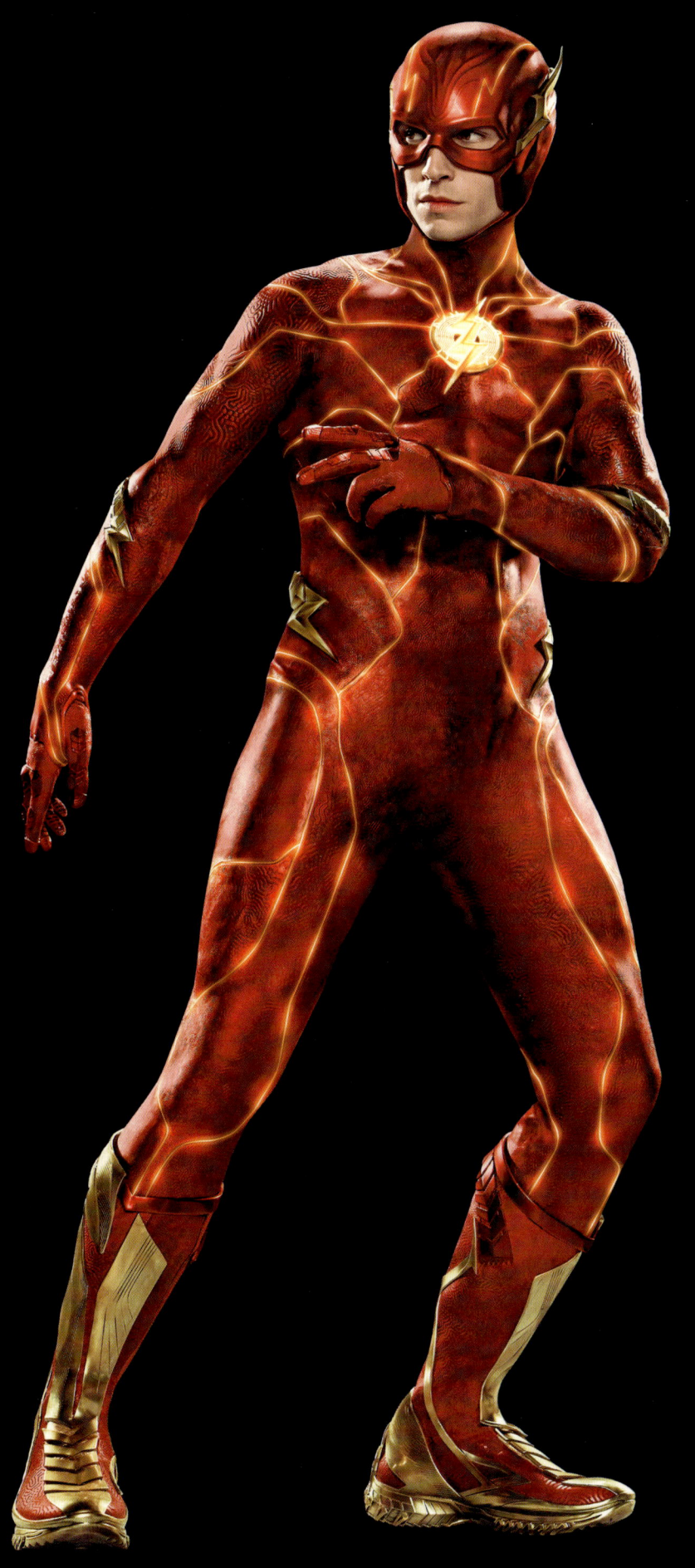

TAILORING THE FLASH

Redesigning The Flash's suit was one of the most exciting aspects of the film for director Andy Muschietti. From a story perspective, he felt Barry would have continued to refine his suit since the events of *Justice League*. Muschietti feels that "given that five years have gone by, The Flash would almost inevitably have a new suit. And considering that he's befriended Bruce Wayne, Bruce would help him, or provide him with a suit that has better technology." Muschietti envisioned a suit that had "an aesthetic that is a little more like the comic books, where the suit is elastic but still has a structure," and features new, visually exciting elements unlike other superhero suits seen in films.

To realize his vision, Muschietti turned to costume designer Alexandra Byrne and costume supervisor Dan Grace, both of whom rose to the challenge. Barry's connection to the Speed Force needed to be felt when he ran. Through the use of elaborate circuitry, channeled lines throughout the suit illuminate as Barry runs. The light is enhanced with postproduction visual effects, but the circuitry built into the suit serves as a starting point. Costume effects supervising modeler Pierre Bohanna recalls that the suit required nearly seven months of research and development. He shares that the suit was "a very dense and complicated piece of work" comprising forty-six components that all had to come together to appear as a single piece—one that's also supposed to appear lightweight and flexible, with a satin texture.

THE FLASH'S RING

Barry Allen's genius extends far beyond the crime lab. Solving perhaps one of the most puzzling aspects of being a Super Hero—where to store your suit when not in use—Barry develops a practical and subtle yet stylish solution. He stores his costume within a hidden compartment in his gold signet ring, which is emblazoned with a lightning bolt. While miniature at first, the suit expands to full size when exposed to atmospheric gases—all faster than the human eye could possibly see. With the ring always on his finger, Barry is prepared to leap into action anywhere he goes! When it's time to change, Barry presses a tiny button on his ring, causing the lightning bolt signet to slide open and eject the suit. The ring is both tasteful and functional, so Barry never needs to run home to get his suit or keep it on beneath his clothing.

THE SUIT AND RING IN TWO DIMENSIONS

In the comics, Barry's suit is made from the same synthetic silk and Teflon, though he developed the fabric on his own while in college. A later version of the suit ejects in pieces and fuses together on his body, with the ring's lightning symbol expanding to become the symbol on his chest.

QUICK CHANGE

Using his speed to put on the suit quickly is to Barry's (and everyone else's) benefit. As cool as it looks seeing the suit expand in the air, once it's released from the ring, it'll quickly flop onto the ground into a pile unless Barry starts moving at super-speed. The key benefit of getting changed at high speeds is that no one will see the unglamorous fumbling that donning a skintight Super Hero suit entails.

THE RING'S COMIC BOOK ORIGIN

Whenever anyone asks him about the curious lightning ring on his finger, Barry can never keep his cover straight. He always seems to have a different story for it, such as that it was his school ring, a gift from his father, or one he received from a police fraternity. In fact, Barry forged it from his parents' wedding rings. It's a reminder of better days and brings Barry hope.

HOW IT WORKS

An ingenious work of engineering, the ring is built with a mechanism that drives out the hydrogen atoms from the suit, causing it to shrink. With a series of carefully calculated folds, the suit fits back into the ring. The suit's rapid compression generates heat and, once it cools inside the ring, creates a vacuum seal, keeping the ring closed.

ECHOES OF THE PAST

Barry's journey to becoming The Flash begins with the shocking death of his mother, Nora. Finding echoes of his own tragic backstory, Bruce Wayne feels a kinship with the young hero, but knows firsthand where that path can lead—being consumed by vengeance rather than giving yourself the time to heal. In *The Flash*, Bruce warns that no good can come from fighting the past. While Barry argues that Bruce's childhood trauma has been fundamental to Batman's success as a hero, Bruce somberly reminds him of the loneliness he feels—his crime fighting has not given him peace.

THE HUMAN FACTOR

Ezra Miller believes there's something universal and human about Barry's story in one way or another. The question of what we could have done differently lives with us all. Barry's story is also one of perseverance, which is one of the character's most prominent traits. He refuses to give up, even to a fault. Barry believes the answer is out there to find, as long as he keeps looking.

NORA ONSCREEN

Nora Allen is exactly the sort of mother a child like Barry Allen needs. She can see the genius behind his eyes, even when he is only eight years old, and how it can overwhelm him. Nora is perfect at assuring him that not every problem has a solution and, sometimes, a person just has to let go.

She shows him how to live in the moment and get out of his own head. Instead of stressing over homework that is, in fact, beneath him, he can find greater joy just making dinner with his mother while she sings along to a Rubén Blades song.

TAKING THE FALL

The idyllic Sunday night dinner takes a heartbreaking turn while Henry is at the store. A stranger breaks into the Allen house, a fight ensues, and Nora is fatally stabbed with her own kitchen knife. Henry returns to the bloody aftermath. It is an unexpected and tragic crime that could have been avoided had the stranger not assumed the house was empty after Henry drove off. With no evidence of an intruder and Barry completely unaware of what transpired while he did his homework upstairs, Henry is arrested for Nora's murder and later convicted, setting in motion Barry's mission to become a crime scene investigator and clear his father's name

A FORCE OF NATURE

Inhabiting a relatively small role, actress Maribel Verdú makes a huge impact as Nora. Her film husband, Ron Livingston, asserts that "her essence just fills the screen. It lights it up. And you really get the sense of how the loss of this vibrant soul is felt." Her performance perfectly conveys the magnitude of the loss Barry feels.

JUST ONE QUICK ERRAND

One errand changes the life of Dr. Henry Allen (Ron Livingston) forever. The Allen family is getting ready for dinner; on Sundays, Henry's wife, Nora (Maribel Verdú), makes her special Sunday Sauce. But this particular day, she needs an extra can of tomatoes, which she forgot to buy that morning. Henry jokes they should send their son, eight-year-old Barry (Ian Loh), on the errand before he ventures out to buy the can of tomatoes himself.

A DOUBLE TRAGEDY

The Allen family is destroyed in more ways than one the night Nora is murdered. When discussing the role of Henry Allen, actor Ron Livingston expresses that "when you're somebody's parent, your life just changes. Your priorities change. It becomes less about you [and] more about this person you're there to take care of. . . . One of the biggest pieces of the tragedy that goes down is that not only does he lose his wife in this horrific manner, not only does he lose his freedom, but he really loses his chance to be Barry's dad." To Livingston, the only reason Henry still goes through with each legal appeal isn't because he thinks he's going to be released, but because the court hearings give him a chance to see his son.

THE ILLUSTRATED LIFE OF NORA ALLEN

Within the pages of The Flash comics, Nora Thompson Allen is a caring and supportive mother to Barry. She extols the virtues of being honest, resilient, kind, and—most important—of slowing down. Barry's love of comic books comes from reading her collection, which he finds stowed away in the attic. Many of Barry's strongest characteristics can be traced back to moments spent with Nora when he was a child.

When Nora debuted in The Flash #126 (February 1962) alongside her husband, Henry, she was alive and well. In the story, Barry returns to his hometown of Fallville, Iowa, to visit them. She and Henry are little more than cameos in this larger story about Barry reuniting with a childhood sweetheart and soon stopping a jewel robbery. She appears a few more times, including at Barry's wedding to Iris. For years, Barry hides his identity as The Flash from Nora and Henry. It isn't until they're involved in a serious car accident, which leaves Nora briefly comatose, and Henry is possessed by the Top, one of The Flash's enemies, that Barry lets his parents in on in on his secret identity. Not long after Barry dies in Crisis on Infinite Earths, Nora and Henry succumb to natural causes and are buried beside him.

In 2009's The Flash: Rebirth comic miniseries, Barry Allen grapples with a feeling of loss he can't explain. He recalls the one case he could never solve, as either The Flash or a CSI—Nora's murder when he was a boy. Barry soon learns his archnemesis, Reverse-Flash, has resorted to even more diabolical tactics in his vendetta against The Flash. Traveling through Barry's past and rewriting history, Reverse-Flash orchestrates a series of tragic events, culminating in Nora's premature death. Not even the memory of Barry's original past remains, just the knowledge that Reverse-Flash took it—and his family—from him.

LETTING GO

Henry accepts the fact that he's going to spend the rest of his life in prison, but worries that Barry's efforts to free him are robbing his son of his own life. Henry wants to see Barry move on and no longer be stuck in the past. Each failed appeal is another distraction, preventing Barry from having a normal life and doing things like finding love. Even if some form of justice is carried out and Henry's conviction overturned, it wouldn't return their lost time to him and Barry, nor will it bring back Nora. Barry must learn that lesson his own way.

EVERLASTING HOPE

Older than his film counterpart, the comic book version of Barry is also a little wiser. He manages to make peace with Nora's death. But that doesn't mean he forgets her. He carries her memory with him each time he suits up as The Flash. Talking to her as though she's still alive, Barry affirms that he didn't become The Flash out of suffering or tragedy. He did it because of what she taught him—because it was the right thing to do.

ACROSS THE MULTIVERSE

Within the pages of *The Flash* #47 in February 2016, Henry's incarceration comes to an end. As The Flash, Barry has fought and defeated the true culprit, Reverse-Flash. Then, in his civilian identity, Barry sees that Reverse-Flash is arrested, and states he could put together the forensic evidence to prove the Super-Villain is guilty. After twenty years behind bars, Henry is free thanks to his son's efforts as both a Super Hero and a CSI.

In the 2014 television series *The Flash*, Barry is also successful in getting his father exonerated, but the happy reunion is short-lived. The villainous Zoom, a Reverse-Flash counterpart from another Earth, kills Henry before Barry's eyes, in the same exact spot where Nora was killed.

Nora (Michelle Harrison) is an inspiring presence in the younger Barry's life in the 2014 TV series. When Young Barry laments not being fast enough to stop bullies from picking on other kids, Nora reminds him that he has a good heart and that "it's better to have a good heart than fast legs." The lightning brought Barry the speed, but without Nora's moral compass he never would've run in the right direction.

INTRODUCING IRIS WEST

A former college classmate of Barry's, Iris West (played in the film by Kiersey Clemons)—now an investigative reporter—reconnects with him as she follows the story of his father's court case.

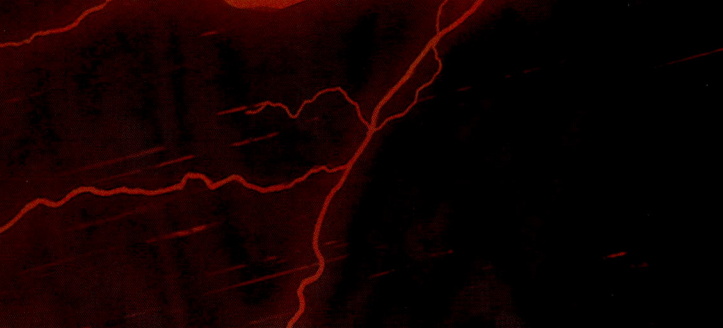

DIGGING DEEP

Iris chose a career in journalism to shine a light on the wrongs in the world and find a way to right them. In that regard, she finds a kindred spirit in Barry. Playing Iris, actress Kiersey Clemons feels that as a journalist, "she'll always want to dig, and I think . . . she is energetically attracted to Barry in that way. She also sees the passion and the vigor that he has to prove what he knows, [and] that inspires her and motivates her." She can make sense of Barry and his oftentimes eccentric ways of thinking and acting. This alone makes her a great ally in his pursuit of justice for his father.

WISE BEYOND HER AGE

Though only twenty-five years old, Iris possesses a greater maturity than her peers. It's a balancing act to do her job well while also showing compassion for Barry as a friend. She does not let her journalistic drive get in the way of her sensitivity. When she's with Barry, Clemons notes, she's "a bit more empathetic, and you see that through the way [she and Barry] interact. It's really special."

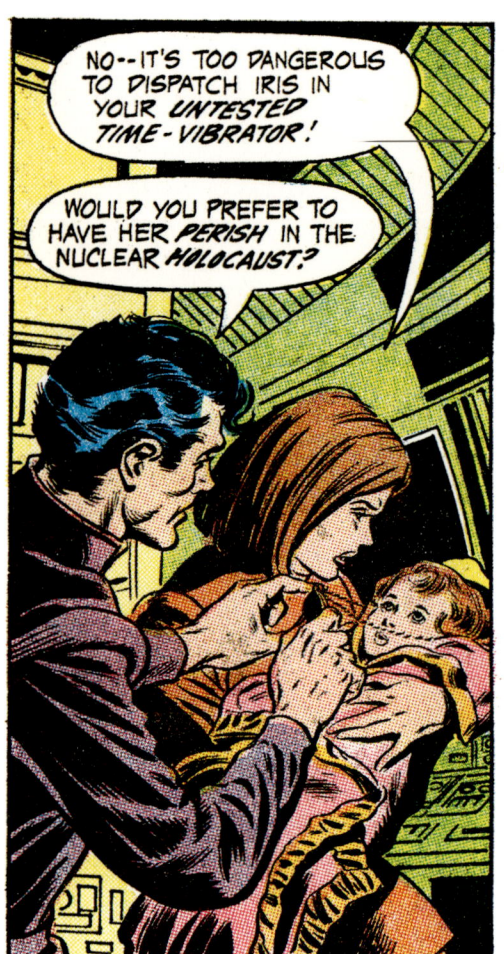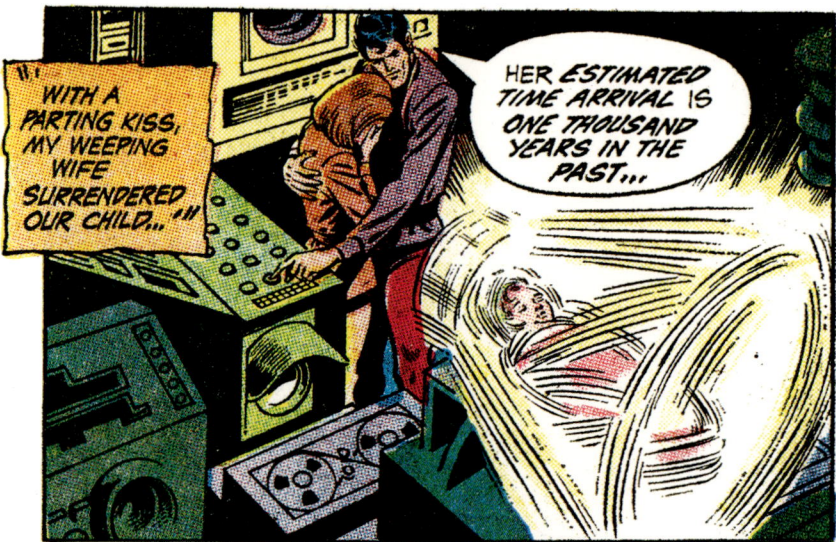

THE ROOTS OF IRIS

Iris West has a unique backstory in the comics. She debuted alongside Barry in *Showcase* #4 as a reporter. But fourteen years later, in February 1971's *The Flash* #203, Iris learns that the people who raised her were not her biological parents. In a stunning reveal, she discovers that her birth parents lived one thousand years in the future and sent her to the past when the world during their time was threatened with nuclear destruction.

Several years after she and Barry are married, Iris is murdered by Reverse-Flash, or so Barry believes. At the moment of her death, her parents in the future use advanced technology to draw her life force back to them. This is described as a psychic transplant, and one of the riskiest medical procedures the thirtieth century could offer, but they are able to put her life force into the body of a woman who has just died of natural causes.

Later reunited with Barry in the thirtieth century, Iris conceives twins, Don and Dawn Allen. She returns to the present day when her grandson Bart is suffering from rapid aging as a result of his genetic connection to the Speed Force. In the present day, she seeks help from her nephew Wally, who has taken over as The Flash. She chooses to remain in the present, where she writes *The Life Story of The Flash*, the definitive account of the life she shared with Barry and his adventures as The Flash.

Much of Iris's history with Barry is lost because of changes in reality, but it should come as no surprise that they find their way back to each other, and many of their memories return.

...BUT BARRY ALLEN NEVER GIVES *ME* THE TIME OF DAY.

IF IT ISN'T *IRIS WEST*.

ACROSS THE MULTIVERSE

On the CW network's television series *The Flash*, which launched in 2014, Iris is portrayed by Candice Patton and shares many of her counterparts' strong qualities. She's the owner and editor in chief of the *Central City Citizen*. She and Barry are married, though their wedding was interrupted by Nazi villains from a parallel Earth. Iris is fiercely protective of Wally (Keiynan Lonsdale)—her brother in this reality, rather than her nephew—and his exploits as Kid Flash. Like her comic incarnation, Iris is always ready to step in and help, taking over as leader of Team Flash, the network of heroes operating in Central City.

WELCOME TO CENTRAL CITY

Central City is a flourishing Midwestern metropolis that has served as The Flash's home since he first donned the red suit. Highly developed, it's filled with skyscrapers, restaurants, chain coffee shops, parks, and a thriving nightlife. Known as the City Always on the Run, Central City also attracts a high volume of metahuman crime.

FINDING THE RIGHT LOOK AND FEEL

The overall aesthetic of Central City was inspired by art deco buildings of the 1920s and '30s. Production designer Paul D. Austerberry wanted it to be visually distinctive from another key DC location, Batman's Gotham City. Jason Knox-Johnston took that idea and depicted Central City as more vibrant, with its parks, outdoor cafés, and other bustling locations. In contrast, Gotham City feels darker, a place in which you might still look over your shoulder. When observing both cities, you'll notice that Central City appears as though it were constructed from brick, while Gotham City looks like its chief building material is concrete. These subtle changes add to the distinctive character of each city.

ON LOCATION

In the movie *The Flash*, Central City is brought to life in London, though you'd never be able to tell. Part of the illusion comes from the way streets are dressed by the film's set decorators. Store signs are changed, as are license plates on the cars. As supervising art director Jason Knox-Johnston shares, "You've got to cover all that kind of stuff up. Anything that's quintessentially London, you've also got to remove. Sometimes, you don't get as much prep time as you'd like, so we do go with our cap in hand to [Visual Effects] to help us out as well, which they graciously do."

PRIME LOCATIONS FROM THE COMICS

Much of Central City has been explored through the comic series *The Flash*, from the bustling downtown to the outer suburbs. In those pages it has a distinct feel compared to other cities, such as Gotham City or Metropolis. Just as those cities were indelibly linked to their Super Heroes Batman and Superman, respectively, Central City is inseparable from The Flash. Here are a few of its most notable locations:

Hidden within The Flash Museum—you'd never find it unless Barry gives you a personal tour—is the **Speed Lab**. Built with twenty-fifth-century technology, the lab provides Barry with means of conducting investigations, as well as tracking his foes and threats in Central City and beyond.

Central City is also home to a branch of **S.T.A.R. Labs** (Science and Technology Advanced Research Laboratories). This state-of-the-art facility specializes in studying the Speed Force, providing additional resources for Barry when needed.

IRON HEIGHTS PENITENTIARY

Located along the waters of the Missouri River is **Iron Heights Penitentiary**, a maximum-security prison that's especially equipped to handle metahuman criminals. It was once seen as impenetrable, and its motto among prisoners and staff is, "The Only Way out of Iron Heights Is in a Body Bag." Warden Gregory Wolfe runs the prison with an iron grip.

GEM CITY BRIDGE

The **Gem City Bridge** spans the Missouri River, connecting Central City to its sister city Keystone City. Once home to a thriving automotive industry, Keystone City is more run-down and economically depressed than its neighbor to the east.

THE FLASH MUSEUM

One of the most exciting attractions within Central City is **The Flash Museum**, dedicated to their great Super Hero and his astonishing legacy. Filled with dramatic multimedia exhibits and displays, the museum is an educational adventure through the life and career of The Flash. Its first curator was Dexter Myles, a former Shakespearean actor who once aided The Flash in stopping a robbery. Proceeds from the museum and its robust gift shop cover operating expenses as well as funding charities, such as The Central City Reclamation Fund and The Flash Memorial Scholarship Fund, a program aiding deserving students at Central City University.

CENTRAL CITY CRIME LAB

The **Central City Crime Lab** is located within the downtown division of the police department and is where you can find Barry—when he makes it to work on time.

BARRY'S CRIME-FIGHTING CAREER

The Central City Crime Lab is where criminal cases are proven or dismissed based on the hard-working efforts of the city's crime scene investigators and their cutting-edge scientific methods. But more than just Barry's place of work, the Crime Lab serves as the birthplace of The Flash. Had Barry not been toiling away in the lab late one night, he never would have been struck by lightning and received his speed powers.

S.T.A.R. LABS SUIT-MAKERS

In the 2014 *The Flash* television series, S.T.A.R. Labs serves as Barry's primary base of operations. Barry's friend, S.T.A.R. Labs scientist Cisco Ramon (Carlos Valdes), creates Barry's suit, first with a reinforced tripolymer material similar to what firefighters wear and, later, as a nanotech-based outfit capable of self-repair and loaded with more features than a smartphone, including the ability to monitor Barry's vital signs from afar. And on Earth-90, where the CBS *The Flash* series that aired in 1990 and 1991 takes place, Dr. Christina "Tina" McGhee (Amanda Pays) of S.T.A.R. Labs provides Barry with his suit, based on a Soviet prototype deep-sea suit. With a layer of reactive insulation, the suit can handle the pressure of high velocities and regulate his body temperature. It also has sensors to keep an eye on Barry's vitals.

OFFICE SPACE

According to Paul D. Austerberry, production designer of the movie *The Flash*, director Andy Muschietti wanted the crime lab to be "kind of an austere, oppressive kind of workplace... Because Barry goes kind of begrudgingly to this job every day, he's in kind of a dour mood. So when we first see this place... it's quite an imposing art deco building." They found the perfect location in the Senate House, located in London's Bloomsbury district, which looks very American and is used as the Crime Lab's exterior.

For the interior, supervising art director Jason Knox-Johnston wanted the lab to feel state-of-the-art and entirely authentic. Working with a forensic technician, the team created a space that was entirely functional. Set decorator Dominic Capon adds that the technician "was super-impressed with all the details. And she just helped us position them and work out how they would be used" so the performers knew how to handle them correctly.

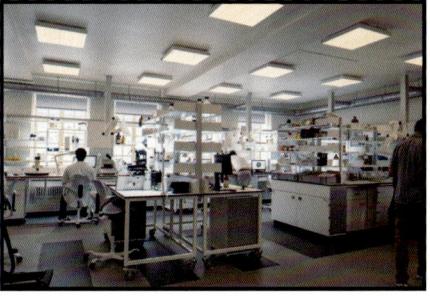

BARRY'S COWORKERS

Albert Desmond (Rudy Mancuso) and Patty Spivot (Saoirse-Monica Jackson) are Barry's colleagues in the Central City Crime Lab. They can get competitive in the lab, but remain available for one another.

THE BOSS

Dr. David Singh (portrayed by Sanjeev Bhaskar) oversees the Cime Lab. He tolerates Barry's frequent tardiness, but only to a point. He wants to see Barry apply himself more and focus on getting through his workload. Closing cases is the measure of success for Dr. Singh, and he's always first to talk to the press about his team's accomplishments.

FAMILIAR FACES FROM THE COMICS

DAVID SINGH

RELATIONSHIP: Colleague
FIRST APPEARANCE: *The Flash* Vol. 4 #1 (November 2011)

David Singh runs the lab in the comics just as he does in the film. Balancing his professional and personal lives isn't always easy, as he struggles to keep secret his relationship with Hartley Rathaway, the reformed Super-Villain known as the Pied Piper. Though he was once primarily focused on closing cases as quickly as possible, regardless of the quality of the work, changes to the timeline have softened his personality, and Singh becomes a more careful and considerate leader.

PATTY SPIVOT

RELATIONSHIP: Colleague
FIRST APPEARANCE: *DC Special Series* #1 (September 1977)

In the comics, Patty Spivot serves as the crime lab's forensic blood analyst. She has long harbored feelings for Barry. In one timeline, they become a couple, but his heart forever belongs to Iris. As capable as she is within the lab, Patty also is the first to rush into harm's way when Central City is in danger. She's fearless, even willing to confront the monstrous Gorilla Grodd to protect an injured Barry.

ALBERT DESMOND

RELATIONSHIP: Colleague
FIRST APPEARANCE: *Showcase* #13 (April 1958)

Albert Desmond has a much more troubled life in the comics. Unlike his film counterpart, the illustrated Albert never gets along with Barry in the lab. He is a brilliant chemist who turns to crime, combining his knowledge of chemistry with the ancient Philosopher's Stone to transmute elements as he grows obsessed with gaining forbidden, mystical knowledge. Known as Doctor Alchemy, Albert eschews the spotlight and seems content to remain incarcerated in Iron Heights Penitentiary, reading centuries-old books, until he finds the motivation to break out, making him one of The Flash's more peculiar foes.

ACROSS THE MULTIVERSE

In the comics, Barry is part of a large family of speedsters. He shares the mantle of The Flash with his former sidekick Wally West. Iris's other nephew, Wallace, takes on the Kid Flash mantle. Barry's speed powers are passed down to his children, Don and Dawn Allen, also known as the Tornado Twins, and his grandchildren, Jenni Ognats (XS) and Bart Allen (Impulse).

Of his fellow Justice League members, Barry maintains a long and close relationship with Hal Jordan, a member of the Green Lantern Corps. They fight side by side for years, in addition to enjoying time together outside of their Super Hero adventures.

THE ORIGINAL CSI

Long before crime scene investigation became a part of popular culture with dozens of police-procedural television series, Barry debuted as a police scientist, which was a precursor to the modern crime scene investigator in comics. It was an entirely different type of police work than what was traditionally depicted. Barry used his smarts rather than a badge and a gun. Given the popularity of CSI work now, Barry was ahead of the curve.

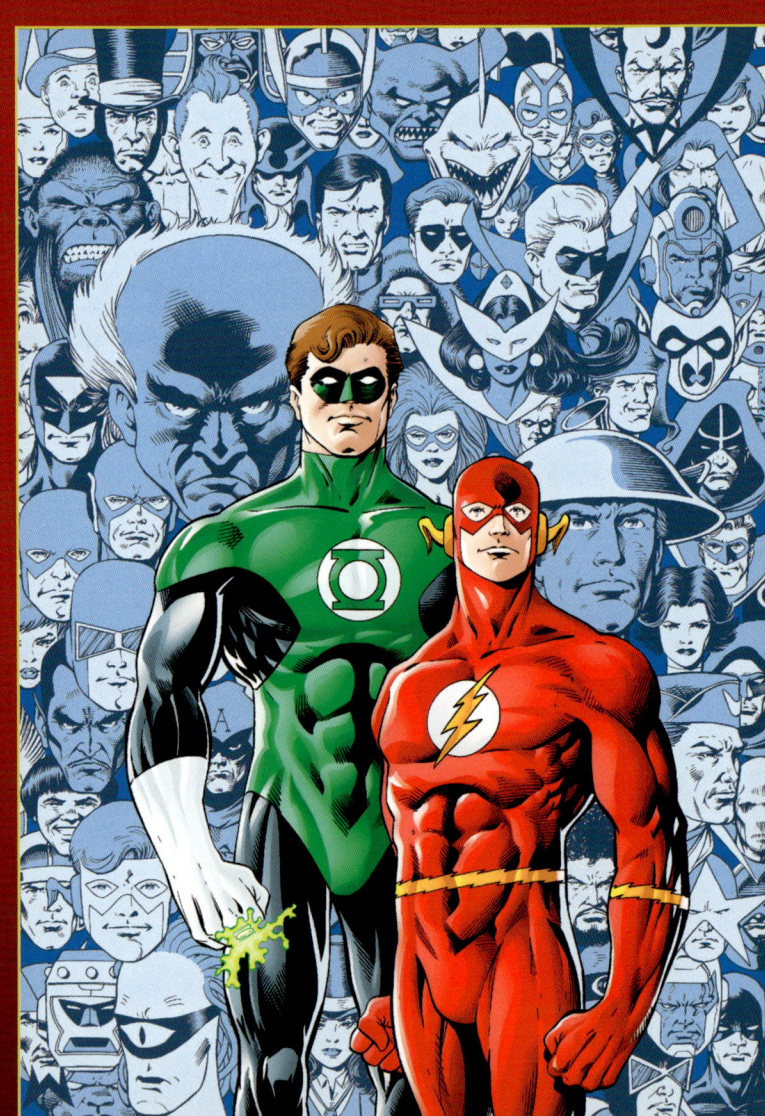

On the CW's *The Flash* series, Barry's two most trusted allies are Cisco Ramon and Dr. Caitlin Snow (Danielle Panabaker). Cisco has the ability to harness dimensional energies as Vibe, and Caitlin possesses ice-based powers as Killer Frost. Over the years, Barry also becomes close with Oliver Queen, the vigilante Green Arrow, and works with other speedsters, like Iris's brother, Wally West (Kid Flash), and Barry's future children, Nora West-Allen (XS) and Bart West-Allen (Impulse).

THE ROGUES GALLERY

Perhaps only second to Batman and the ruthless criminals he has locked away away in Arkham Asylum, The Flash has one of the most colorful and eclectic arrays of villains ever seen on the page and onscreen. These baddies leave Barry with his hands full in *The Flash* comics every month.

THE ROGUES

Led by Captain Cold, the Rogues set out to prove there can be honor among thieves. First appearing as a team in *The Flash* #155 (August 1965), they adhere to a strict moral code that forbids drug use and the killing of speedsters, Super Heroes, women, and children. Their focus is always on the heist at hand. Key members of the Rogues include Heat Wave, Golden Glider, Mirror Master, Trickster, Captain Boomerang, and Weather Wizard, though others have come and gone over the years.

PROFESSOR ZOOM, REVERSE-FLASH

Since his debut in *The Flash* #139 (September 1963), Eobard Thawne has been obsessed with Barry Allen. Hailing from the twenty-fifth century, he turns himself into a speedster and travels back to meet Barry. But his hero quickly becomes his archenemy, and, ever since, Thawne has dedicated his life to ruining Barry's, in the cruelest ways imaginable.

GORILLA GRODD

Superintelligent. Telepathic. Despotic. The ruler of Gorilla City is one of The Flash's most formidable foes and has menaced the speedster since *The Flash* #106 (May 1959). Well aware of the power of the Speed Force, Grodd wants to steal it from Barry and wield it for himself.

ABRA KADABRA

The stage magician known as Citizen Abra takes the award for traveling the farthest, coming all the way from the sixty-fourth century to make problems for Barry. He uses highly advanced technology under the guise of "magic" to commit crimes, starting in *The Flash* #128 (May 1962).

THE TURTLE

The first Super-Villain Barry ever faces, in *Showcase* #4, the Turtle (originally known as the Turtle Man), is the Super Hero's polar opposite. Just as Barry is a conduit to the Speed Force, the Turtle is connected to the Still Force, another of the dominant energies that make up the universe.

THE FLASH IN ACTION

The film's action jolts to life like a flash of lightning. Batman calls The Flash to Gotham City for an emergency: A criminal group led by Al Falcone has broken into a high-security research laboratory located beneath Gotham General Hospital and stolen a weaponized virus powerful enough to wipe out half of Gotham City in hours. In their escape, they detonate an explosive that creates a giant sinkhole and has the hospital on the verge of collapse. Batman is in pursuit of the criminals and needs The Flash to help with the collateral damage at the hospital.

SPEED FILMING

When Barry is moving at super-speed, the world appears to be in slow motion. To create this effect, scenes were filmed at varying frame rates (the number of frames, or images, that will compose a single second of footage). Most films are shot at twenty-four frames per second. Ezra Miller was filmed at forty-eight frames per second when Barry is in action, creating a heightened sense of reality without any blurring that would be present at a lower frame rate. But from Barry's perspective, everything around him has slowed down. Second unit director Robert Alonzo notes, "All Ezra's movements, all the action for The Flash, was shot at forty-eight frames, while we're shooting all the ancillary action at six hundred frames, and matching that together to make it all succinct to one sequence. It's definitely a challenge." When the footage is combined, we see Barry moving at one speed while his environment moves at another. In these moments, the audience experiences the world just as Barry does.

THE BABY SHOWER

As the hospital begins to collapse into the sinkhole, The Flash must rescue some of the hospital's most vulnerable patients: babies. He looks up just in time to see a dozen babies, along with a nurse, falling from the windows of the thirtieth-floor nursery. Barry bolts up the side of the building as though gravity has no effect on him. He dodges broken glass and falling medical equipment as he races to reach the infants, all of whom float in the air surrounded by increasingly dangerous objects. The moment is simultaneously nail-biting and playful as we observe Barry problem-solve the dilemma in hyper-speed.

Set decorator Dominic Capon notes director Andy Muschietti's love of practical effects. "He's very tactile," Capon says. "He likes to engage with [the set]." The special effects team constructed the nursery on set, with the room capable of tilting twenty degrees to capture the falling action. Meanwhile, Ezra Miller was hoisted up on wires for his gravity-defying run.

The scene was filmed with a combination of dummies and actual babies, who were closely monitored throughout filming. Second unit director Robert Alonzo claims it was a unique experience, as he had never filmed with babies before. But each one needed to be scanned so they could be added to the finished scene. He says, "Some babies... were just in their bassinets. Some of them were being picked up. Some of them, we just let them sleep. And then, taking those elements, [we put] them in an action sequence where a building is basically falling to the ground. When you're seeing it, you can see how scary it is, but you can also see, through Barry's eyes and Barry's vision, how lighthearted that can be."

BATMAN HITS THE ROAD

While Batman is known for his nighttime patrols of Gotham City, *The Flash* opts to show him in a brand-new light—daylight. Batman's pursuit of the criminals occurs during the busy morning commuting hours, forcing him to contend with traffic and bystanders everywhere as he chases the terrorists through the streets of Gotham City. With Glasgow as the filming location for Gotham City, Andy Muschietti wanted as much of the chase as possible to be filmed on the actual streets.

Debuting in the film is a brand-new Batcycle. Muschietti told production designer Paul Austerberry he wanted a motorcycle built like a tank, massive in size and capable of ramming other vehicles. Special effects supervisor Dominic Tuohy explains the collaboration in making the bike, saying, "This is where Special Effects and Visual Effects work hand-in-hand, because we only have X amount of time to build that bike.... I think we had ten weeks in total to build [it]." Using an electric motorbike as the basis, they constructed the large Batcycle, which was nearly ten feet long and three feet wide. Despite its size, it could drive over eighty miles per hour. Tuohy says, "When you see that weaving through the streets, that movement that you see is real." Approximately 85 percent of the Batcycle's effects and functions were practical instead of relying on CGI. Everyone involved was thrilled with the results, with supervising art director Jason Knox-Johnston sharing, "[Tuohy] was very insistent that it should be real, and it was well worth the effort. It looked fantastic."

Nico Ferrari, the picture vehicles coordinator, and Nick Murray, the picture vehicles supervisor, had their own challenge for the thrilling sequence. The terrorists' getaway vehicle is a Humvee, but that type of vehicle isn't built for a high-speed city chase, where it needs to drift and slide. So Ferrari and Murray had to build their own. They stripped down a Ford F-150 Lightning pickup truck to its engine, gear box, and wheels, and then built it back up with a new fiberglass body created by Tuohy and his crew. Onscreen it looks identical to a Humvee, but it can perform like no other.

With the Batcycle and the Humvee ready for the road, Robert Alonzo had to map out the route of the chase. He likened the process to playing chess, charting the paths of not just the Batcycle and the Humvee, but also those of every vehicle and person that came into contact with them as they raced through Glasgow.

THE SPEED FORCE

Beyond the speed of light lies a cosmic force that gives speedsters like Barry their power. Barry dubs it the Speed Force and explains it to Bruce Wayne when they first meet in the 2017 movie Justice League: "It's like this layer of dimensional reality, and it seems to manipulate space-time." The Speed Force alters Barry's body at a genetic level, and he must consume massive amounts of food to make up for all the calories he burns in super-speed. As The Flash begins, Barry is just scratching the surface of the near-limitless potential of the Speed Force.

TAPPING INTO THE SOURCE

The comics show that the Speed Force is an extradimensional field that pushes both space and time forward. In essence, it's reality in motion. All speedsters, including Barry Allen, tap into the excess energy it produces, drawing their velocity from it. It's all-encompassing—an energy that exists in every dimension, universe, and era. It touches every part of reality and contains the knowledge of every place and time.

When speedsters run too fast, they risk being absorbed into the Speed Force. Without an anchor—like a loved one—to pull them back, they could become lost within its massive energy. It hosts the spirits of multiple speedsters who have breached its barrier and become stuck there. To harness the Speed Force means to commune with others who wielded it. But a connection to the Speed Force

is not always a gift. It could be volatile and manifest in unpredictable ways. In the comics, Barry's grandson suffers from rapid aging as a result of his inability to control his powers, appearing to be twelve years old by the time he's two.

Within the comics the Speed Force proves to be as mysterious as it is powerful. Barry Allen's protégé Wally West is the first speedster to enter the Speed Force and manage to return. Barry himself becomes trapped in the Speed Force after his sacrifice during *Crisis on Infinite Earths*. It isn't until Barry's return that the true origin of the Speed Force is revealed.

Like other speedsters, Barry assumes he has tapped into the Speed Force the night he's struck by lightning. In fact, in that moment, he creates it. Barry is the engine generating the kinetic and temporal energy that encapsulates the Speed Force and exists in all time periods at once. Speedsters from both the past and the future have Barry to thank for their abilities; they've harnessed the energy he generates with every step.

THE ORIGIN OF THE SPEED FORCE

The concept of the Speed Force was first introduced during writer Mark Waid's seminal *The Flash* run in the 1990s. The current Flash, Wally West, found himself locked in super-speed, watching the entire world move in slow motion. Max Mercury, another speedster, helped him out of the predicament and explained that it occurred because Wally had further tapped into the Speed Force.

Mark Waid conceived of the Speed Force to reconcile the various ways the speed-powered characters gained their abilities in the DC universe. While Barry and Wally gained their speed under similar circumstances, the others had different origins. The Golden Age Flash Jay Garrick inhaled hard-water fumes and woke up with his speed, for example. Johnny Quick, however, recited a formula—3×2(9YZ)4A—in order to run. But Waid decided that regardless of the situation, all speedsters were tapping into this single force. From that moment on, the Speed Force was a key component in nearly every major *The Flash* storyline.

THE POWER OF SPEED

Barry's connection to the Speed Force offers much more than swift legs. Throughout his career as The Flash, he unlocks numerous special abilities. Ezra Miller shares that what they love most about Barry as a Super Hero is that speed is "theoretically just a singular power . . . but then, combined with the intelligence of a speedster, that one factor, when pushed to extremes, means so many different capacities, capabilities, and powers." In the comics, Barry displays many of these extraordinary abilities.

⚡ AIR MANIPULATION

With the spin of his arms, Barry can manipulate the air in a variety of ways. He can create condensed bursts of air to knock crooks off their feet or small vortexes to sweep them up into the sky in small, controlled tornados. Or, if Barry himself is falling from a great height, he can whip up an air cushion to break his fall.

⚡ ALONG FOR THE RIDE

In a pinch, Barry can take anything he needs along with him. The Speed Force acts as a tether, pulling objects in his slipstream, from another person to two 600-ton boats.

⚡ THE SKY'S THE LIMIT

Barry's powers appear limitless at times. He can emit electrical blasts and blinding lights, heal quickly, give and borrow speed, and block telepaths from accessing his mind. With master control over his body, if there's something Barry can think of doing, he'll figure out how to do it.

⚡ FAST THINKING

Barry's brain processes all information around him simultaneously. At super-speed, he can see all possible outcomes, weighing them and deciding how to act accordingly before anyone notices that anything is wrong.

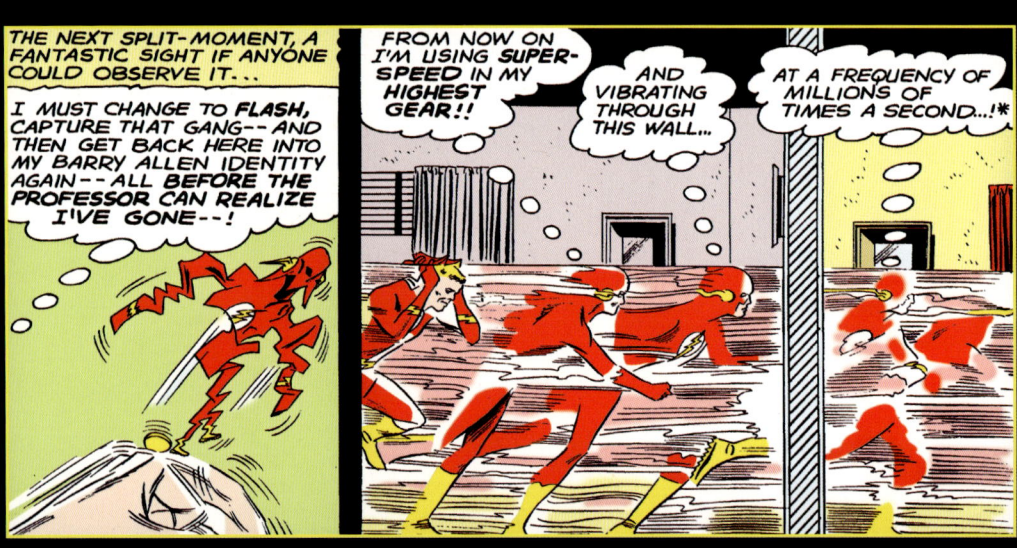

⚡ JUST A PHASE

A solid object is no obstacle for Barry. With perfect control over the atoms and molecules in his body, Barry can slip through anything solid, even a steel wall, as though it were nothing.

⚡ CLOUD HOPPING

Who needs the ability to fly when Barry can simply skip from cloud to cloud in the sky?

⚡ SPEED READING

Research is never an issue for Barry, who consumes the knowledge of entire libraries in less time than it takes a regular person to turn a single page.

⚡ SOLID SURFACES NOT REQUIRED

Barry can also run on water as though it's solid ground. With his nimble footwork, he can cross oceans when necessary, without ever getting wet.

BARRY'S NATURAL GIFTS

Barry was full of talent even before he was struck by lightning. He showed great intellect, even at a young age. And, as he tells Bruce Wayne upon their first meeting in the film *Justice League*, he's proficient in viola playing and web design, and is fluent in gorilla sign language.

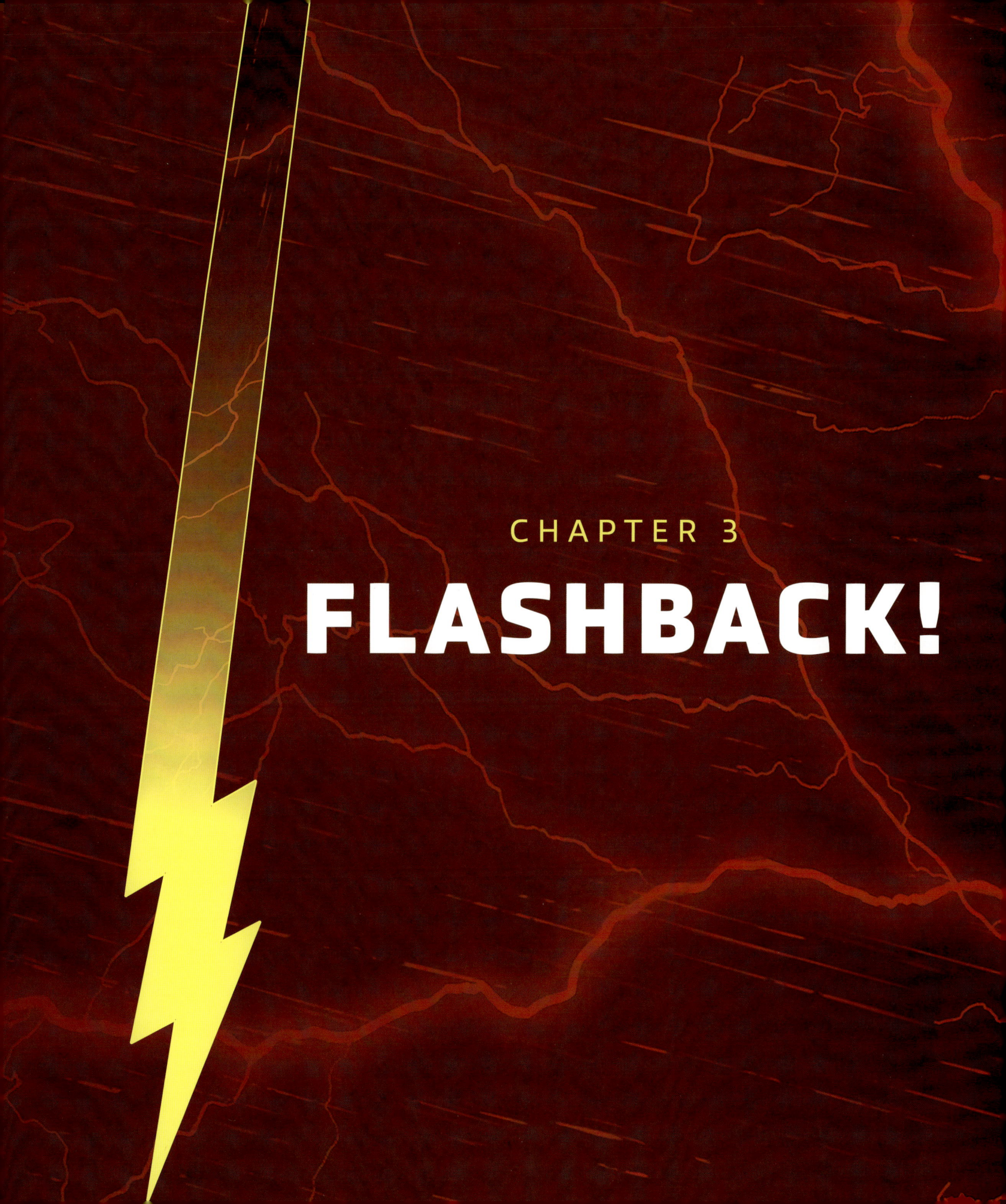

DISCOVERING THE CHRONOBOWL

In the film The Flash, after having failed to turn up new evidence to exonerate his father in the latest court appeal, Barry channels his frustration and grief into speed by taking off running. He pushes himself faster than ever before as he zooms out of the city. Traveling faster than the speed of light, Barry sees the world as he knows it fade away and finds himself in a new and unexpected location.

THIS IS YOUR LIFE, BARRY ALLEN

In a stadium-like sphere, Barry can see all his memories, his entire life, captured in rings. The rings nearest to him are his most recent memories. Each row contains a different set of memories, building out and upward, with his most distant memories at the greatest distance. Every memory is seen through Barry's point of view; everything is subjective, drawn from what he experienced in the past. But the Chronobowl, as Barry calls it, isn't just a museum of memories; it's a gateway to each one. Passing through the shimmering membrane of the Chronobowl, Barry can step into any moment of his past.

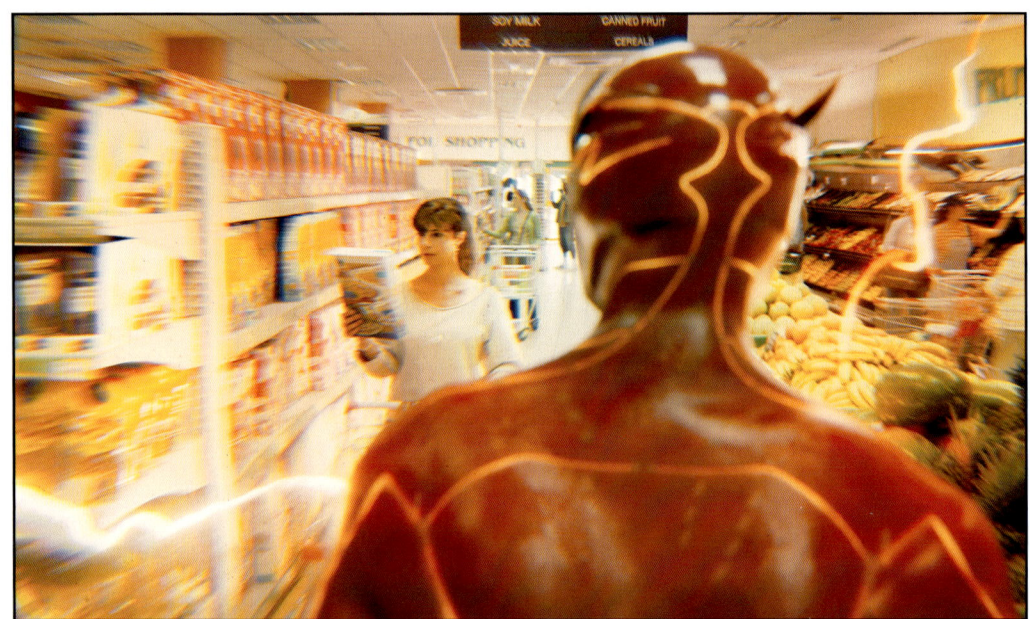

THE QUICK FIX

With his newfound discovery of time travel, Barry is convinced he can save his mother and spare his father a life in prison. Bruce Wayne tells Barry that the effects of altering time would be catastrophic, but Barry refuses to heed Bruce's warning. Barry believes his logic and plan are foolproof. Nora's unknown killer broke into the house because he thought it was empty. Henry wasn't home because Nora sent him out to purchase a can of tomatoes she forgot to buy while food shopping. If Nora hadn't needed the tomatoes, Henry wouldn't have gone out and the murderer never would have broken in. All Barry needs to do is travel back to 2003 and sneak the can of tomatoes into his mother's shopping cart. No one would know he was ever there. But he should know nothing is that simple.

BLAST TO THE PAST

The Chronobowl we see onscreen was born from director Andy Muschietti's desire to create a captivating and innovative way to travel through time. To accomplish this feat, new technology was required. Using a photorealistic technique called volumetric capture, each one of Barry's memories within the Chronobowl is presented in three dimensions. Every aspect of an actor's performance and appearance is perfectly captured and can be viewed from any angle, allowing the camera to move around and through the memories freely. Never before used at this scale in a film, volumetric capture allowed Muschietti to present a new type of movie magic.

MAKING NEW MEMORIES

Barry realizes that the Chronobowl gives him the opportunity not only to step into memories from his past, but also to interact with them. With this knowledge, Barry believes that he can slip in and out of the past without directly interacting with anyone—nobody would know the difference. Moving at super-speed, he rushes through the grocery store, his mom appearing frozen as he maneuvers at his lightning pace. Hoping that this one can of tomatoes will make the difference, Barry travels back through the Chronobowl in one of the film's most heartbreaking moments. As he races back to the present and his new life, with Nora alive, he sees new memories begin to form within the Chronobowl of the life he would have lived if Nora hadn't died. There are birthday parties, family trips, and school graduations. More important, his father is no longer in jail. In fact, he never went to jail. The emotions swell in Barry's eyes as he realizes he has succeeded in fixing the past—until he discovers the cost.

FIRST TRIP TO THE FUTURE

Time travel has been part of the The Flash's mythology from the beginning. In the second of two stories featured in *Showcase* #4, Barry faces Mazdan, a criminal from the distant future, and runs the villain back to his proper time period.

SECOND FIRST TRIP TO THE FUTURE

When Barry receives a new origin story within the pages of 2019's *The Flash: Year One* storyline, his first trip to the future goes a little differently. While testing the limits of his abilities, Barry inadvertently time-travels for the very first time and meets his future self. From the older Barry, he learns he will become a Super Hero known as The Flash. It's an astonishing revelation, as Barry believes being a Super Hero is far outside his comfort zone, and prefers to stick to lab work.

LIFE ON THE RUN

After a battle with Reverse-Flash, Barry finds himself trapped in the realm of Limbo in April 1980's *The Flash* #284. Chased by the realm's master, the Lord of Limbo, Barry runs through all the events of his own life, starting with seeing his birth (he was born two weeks overdue, naturally) before outrunning the Lord of Limbo and returning to the present.

INTRODUCING THE COSMIC TREADMILL

In the pages of December 1961's *The Flash* #125, Barry debuts perhaps his greatest invention: the Cosmic Treadmill. With this device, Barry can reliably travel to any era, past or future. He and Kid Flash use the treadmill to stop alien invaders, the Dokris, in the year 2287. Part of their mission requires Kid Flash to go all the way back to 100,842,246 BCE. Barry later modifies the Cosmic Treadmill to allow for traveling between Earths in the Multiverse in addition to traveling through time.

BRIEFLY HAPPILY EVER AFTER

After being cleared for the murder of Reverse-Flash (it's a long story—and, of course, Reverse-Flash doesn't stay dead), Barry disappears for a time, only to reappear shortly before his death in *Crisis on Infinite Earths*. Where was he? In *The Flash* #350 (July 1985), we see Barry briefly retire to the thirtieth century upon learning that Iris West is alive and well in the future. Barry and Iris spend a month or two together before he puts on the suit once more and heads out to meet his fate.

FLASHPOINT

The film's plotline involving Barry altering the timeline to save his mother's life takes inspiration from the now-classic Flashpoint comic book miniseries by Geoff Johns and Andy Kubert. His attempt to prevent her death results in in a critical flashpoint with numerous unintended consequences. Though Barry has the ability to travel through time, he learns the hard way about the responsibility that comes with such a gift.

THE ORIGINAL FLASHPOINT

The 2011 comic book miniseries began with Barry discovering that his powers are gone and, even more shocking, that his mother, Nora, is alive. But that's not all. There's no one named The Flash, nor is there a Justice League. In this reality, Thomas Wayne becomes Batman after watching his son Bruce get killed. Aquaman and Wonder Woman are locked in a battle that endangers the entire planet. As a child, Superman was taken away by the government to be studied, known only as Subject One. Only Cyborg remains as a beacon of hope, known in this reality as America's greatest hero.

Barry is convinced Reverse-Flash is responsible for this new timeline and enlists Thomas Wayne to help him restore his powers. But Barry soon learns he has only himself to blame. He created this new reality by traveling back in time to prevent Reverse-Flash from murdering his mother. And the only way to set things right is to prevent himself from doing so.

DRAWING INSPIRATION FROM FLASHPOINT

In the film, something as small as a can of tomatoes has a far greater impact than Barry ever anticipated. His mother is alive and his father free of prison, but at a cost. He soon learns that altering the timeline doesn't just change the future. Like when a stone is dropped in a pond, the ripples flow out in all directions, changing the future *and* the past. The Justice League no longer exists. Aquaman was never born. Wonder Woman never left Themyscira. Victor Stone never suffered the accident that turned him into Cyborg. No one has ever heard of Superman. And Batman is a relic of the past, having cleaned up Gotham City. In the absence of heroes, the world is unprotected and completely vulnerable to General Zod's impending attack.

ACROSS THE MULTIVERSE

In 2013, Warner Bros. released an animated film titled *Justice League: The Flashpoint Paradox*. This largely faithful, though condensed, adaptation of *Flashpoint* set the stage for the studio's slate of interconnected animated films that explored the reality created in the wake of Barry's meddling with time.

The 2014 TV series *The Flash* kicked off its third season with its own spin on *Flashpoint*. Distraught by his father's death in the present, Barry travels back in time and saves Nora from being killed by Reverse-Flash. Back in the present, he still has his powers but soon learns he's no longer needed; this reality has its own Flash, Iris's brother Wally. When Wally is critically injured, Barry realizes he's running out of time to set things right. By allowing Reverse-Flash to kill Nora, he's able to restore the timeline, albeit with changes to those around him, including Iris being estranged from her father. Barry is convinced he can fix everything, until a visit from Jay Garrick, The Flash (John Wesley Shipp) from another reality, who explains that things will never be the same. Barry will have to live with the consequences of meddling with time and move forward.

A TALE OF TWO BARRYS

After saving his mother's life in the past, Barry heads back to the present. But he doesn't realize at first that he hasn't quite made it all the way back. While enjoying dinner with his parents in this new timeline, he is shocked to see a younger, powerless version of himself walking toward the house.

YOUNG BARRY

Eighteen-year-old Barry has suffered none of the trauma of his older counterpart. He grew up in a house full of love with both his parents around, and it shows. Producer Barbara Muschietti remarks, "He is spoiled but happy." There's a wide-eyed innocence to him, which he maintains as the original Barry draws him into the action. But when Barry attempts to ensure that his younger self receives his powers in the lab accident, he accidentally loses his own speed in the process. Once Young Barry receives speed powers, he also has the benefit of learning from the best—himself. But that's not to say he masters his abilities right away. Young Barry must learn the hard way that normal clothing won't survive super-speed.

DOUBLE TAKES

To present two Barrys onscreen, the filmmakers used the same volumetric capture technology utilized for the Chronobowl. Many films have featured actors pulling double duty with dual roles, but when three-quarters of the shots in *The Flash* needed to feature both Barrys, director Andy Muschietti had to find a way to free the camera and not overburden production. After numerous tests, the team found a way to use volumetric capture, allowing Ezra Miller to perform as one of the Barrys against a double and then enact the other performance. The two performances were then seamlessly combined.

SAME BUT DIFFERENT

Andy Muschietti brainstormed with Ezra Miller about how they were going to play Young Barry differently, with subtleties and nuances to express how the same character would act after having grown up under different circumstances. Actor Ron Livingston pointed out that both Henry and Barry are affected in an unexpected way by the change in the timeline. Both Young Barry and his father are a little lighter, even goofier, because they've never faced the trauma from the original timeline. Because of that, Livingston says, "they haven't grown."

HOME MAKEOVER

Beyond the actors' performances, the film's crew worked their own subtleties to convey the different timelines. Most notably, these changes could be found in Barry's apartment. Production designer Paul D. Austerberry and supervising art director Jason Knox-Johnston dressed the same space in two different ways to express the contrast between the two Barrys. Knox-Johnston notes that in the original timeline, the apartment is "very Spartan [and] it's falling apart," because Barry is too preoccupied to care for it. It is just a place for Barry to rest and work on proving his father's innocence. Austerberry points out that he and his team "didn't just dial down the color, we painted it differently. We grayed out all the greens, [and] the decor was very different." Cinematographer Henry Braham used colder lighting to add to the effect. But Young Barry's apartment feels more like a home. It expresses Young Barry's comfortable lifestyle. And, most important, this Barry has roommates, filling the space with life. Knox-Johnston adds, "It's a place you want to stay."

ACROSS THE MULTIVERSE

Young Barry isn't the first alternate self the original Barry encounters. During the CW's "Crisis on Infinite Earths" crossover event in 2019, the film and television worlds collide when Ezra Miller meets their TV counterpart Grant Gustin. The circumstances involve the film's Barry briefly finding himself in the S.T.A.R. Labs headquarters of television's Barry. They take an immediate liking to each other before Ezra Miller's Barry fades away.

RECAPTURING LIGHTNING

One of the most iconic images from the *Flashpoint* comic is carried over to the film. Without his powers, Barry must attempt to replicate the circumstances of his initial accident in a last-ditch effort to gain his powers. With the help of Batman and a homemade electric chair that looks like it came out of an old horror movie, Barry braces for more jolts of lightning. It's yet another moment that captures the extent of Barry's perseverance. Although the experiment seems to fail, Barry insists on fighting through the pain until he finally gets his powers back.

RAIN SOAKED HAIR
ENTRY WOUND
EXIT WOUND

Makeup designer Victoria Down delighted in the opportunity this scene offered in creating the look of a lightning-struck Barry. In her research, she discovered that lightning strikes leave a burn that's shaped like a tree of little lightning bolts. Upon her discovery, she says, "I built it in about thirty pieces of prosthetic and convinced Ezra [Miller], who loved it, and Andy [Muschietti] that we would turn it into the tree of life and put it on [Barry's] chest and all the way down him so that when he's lying there and we think he's dying, he's got this incredibly beautiful lightning burn based on reality."

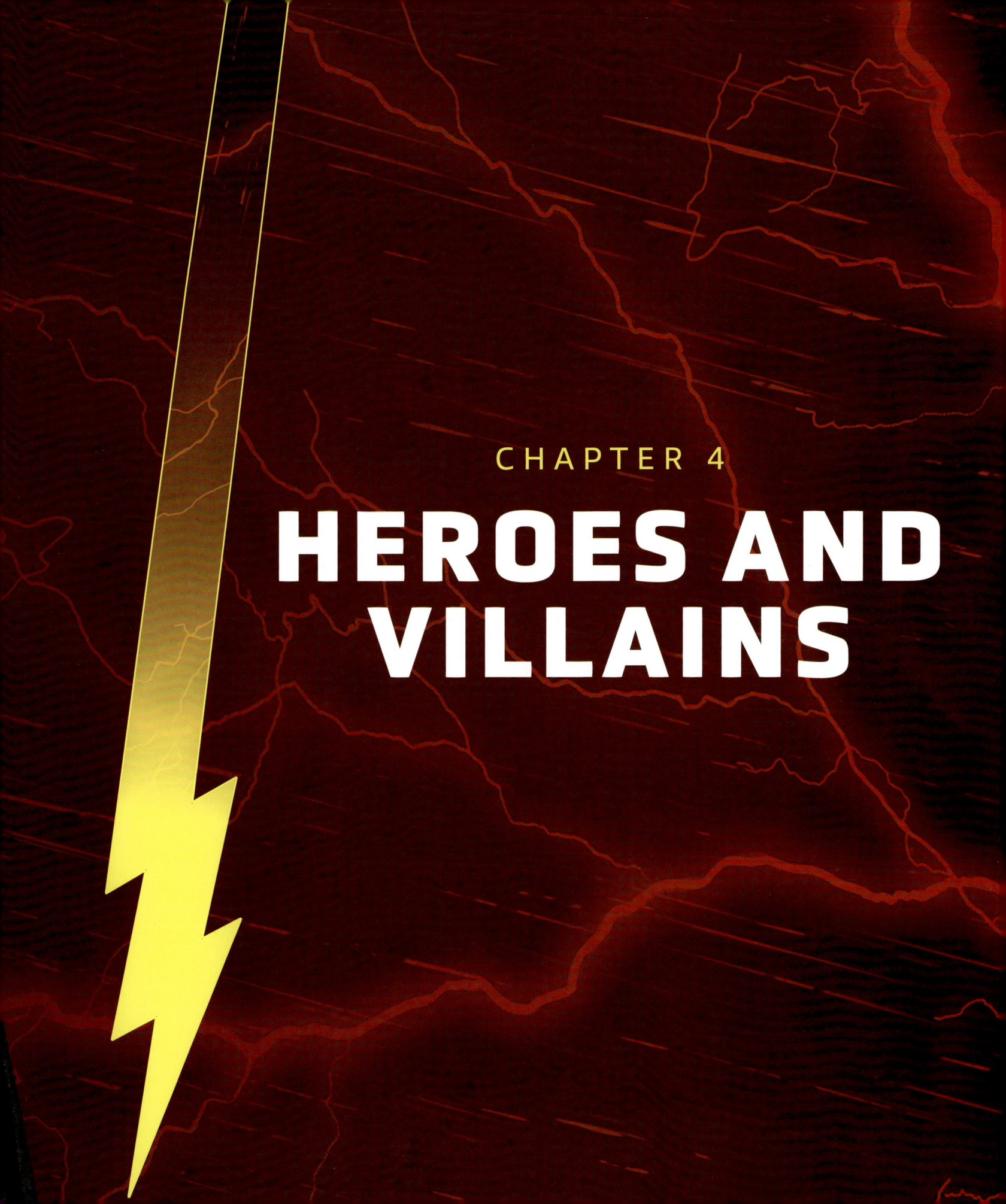

THE DARK KNIGHT RETURNS

If anyone is going to help Barry defeat Zod, it's going to be Batman. Barry is relieved to learn Batman still exists in this new timeline. But once he arrives at Wayne Manor, he is in for yet another surprise.

HE'S BATMAN

Michael Keaton's portrayal of the Dark Knight in Tim Burton's *Batman* (1989) and *Batman Returns* (1992) set the bar for Super Hero performances. The way he embodies the dual roles of Batman and Bruce Wayne remains unrivaled. Director Andy Muschietti has a deep admiration for Keaton, having grown up watching his films. The chance to bring that incarnation of Batman back and explore how he's changed over the past three decades excited Muschietti a great deal. Keaton was quick to answer the call of the Bat-Signal once more. The director shares, "There was not a lot of convincing, because I think Michael Keaton was very enthusiastic about playing Bruce Wayne and Batman again. There were a lot of nuances, of course, about what is Bruce Wayne, you know, twenty-five years later, thirty years later, after we saw him for the last time." Producer Barbara Muschietti adds that Keaton "has been an amazing partner.... No one knows the Tim Burton *Batman* as well as he does."

TWILIGHT OF THE BAT

Unlike the Batman of Barry's original timeline, this Bruce Wayne has done the unimaginable—he's retired. After helping to make Gotham into one of the safest cities in the world, Bruce knows his job is done. Gotham no longer needs him, so he retreats into Wayne Manor and becomes a recluse. Bruce is reluctant to help Barry, but the power and allure of wearing the Batsuit one more time proves to be too tempting. As he tells Barry before they head out to stop Zod, "You wanna get nuts?" He is ready to go out fighting.

WAYNE MANOR THEN AND NOW

In 1989's *Batman*, two houses located about twenty-five miles north of London served as Wayne Manor. Knebworth House, a Gothic-Tudor mansion in Stevenage, was used for the exteriors and many of the interior scenes, while Hatfield House in Hertfordshire served as the location for many of the interiors. It was important for Andy Muschietti and the film's design crew to provide a visual and emotional connection to Keaton's performances in the earlier films. Production designer Paul D. Austerberry reveals that the crew returned to Knebworth House to film at its gate, but story elements in *The Flash* required a taller mansion with an expansive rooftop for a critical scene. They found this at the massive Burghley House in Stamford. Austerberry says it offered a "very similar Elizabethan kind of exterior [where] the stone color matched the gate, [with] the most interesting rooftop out of all these stately homes."

Set decorator Dominic Capon loved being able to return to Hatfield House as the interior setting of Wayne Manor. As he re-created rooms like the armory, he was able to put his own spin on them. Seeing Barry walking through the armory, the audience is drawn back to the moment when Bruce Wayne first meets Vicki Vale in the same space in *Batman*. Capon carefully curated this rebuilt armory, sharing that "we've got a bit of a license to play with some ideas here and take it a bit further, [as though] Bruce had carried on collecting" in the ensuing decades.

75

JOURNEY INTO THE BATCAVE

The Batcave in *Batman* was partially realized using miniatures and matte paintings. For this film, with a larger budget as well as a larger studio, Paul D. Austerberry and his team were able to build a massive 360-degree environment. He kept the elements that make the cave immediately recognizable, but, by building it out, created a space that feels fully immersive. Austerberry was also able to show parts of the Batcave that audiences have never seen before, such as a big hydroelectric power turbine that supplies the electricity needed to sustain the Batcave in addition to Wayne Manor.

Dominic Capon and his team drew inspiration from the films *Batman* and *Batman Returns*, taking note of how the Batcave was dressed. Capon says, "We studied the films very closely and looked at what they'd done in the dressing sense, and it was lovely. It was very original for its time, and I didn't want to throw the baby out with the bathwater. I really wanted to embrace what they'd done but then upgrade it and give it a new twist and slightly modernize, as Batman would have done." Prop modeler Emily Bick and her crew expertly re-created such aspects of the Batcave as Batman's control desk while adding just the slightest of updates. To complete the picture, Austerberry says, the director "wanted the whole Batcave to be covered in dust and dirt and bat guano." Every console and dial needed to feel untouched and abandoned for decades.

BATMAN'S WONDERFUL TOYS

Hidden behind a wall in Bruce's library lies a compartment storing multiple Batsuits—varied in design and function—along with an array of weaponry and gadgets, all calling back to the ones first designed by John Evans for the original films. Batman's Utility Belts, spearguns, grappling hooks, and Batarangs all adorn the walls.

Costume effects supervising modeler Pierre Bohanna loved the experience of creating the different Batsuits. Since they were built as display models, none of them needed to be functional. He shares, "It was great fun to merge between our prop making and our costume making. We could use the best of both." The suits range from what appears to be Batman's very first suit to ones meant for flying and diving and one that is clearly influenced by the blue-and-gray suit from Batman comic books.

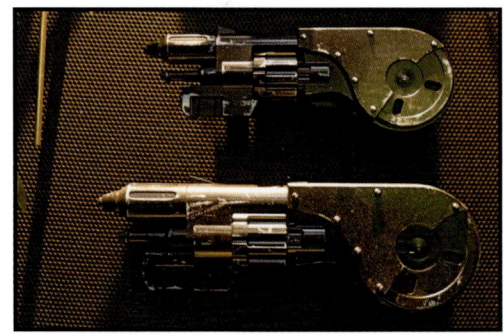

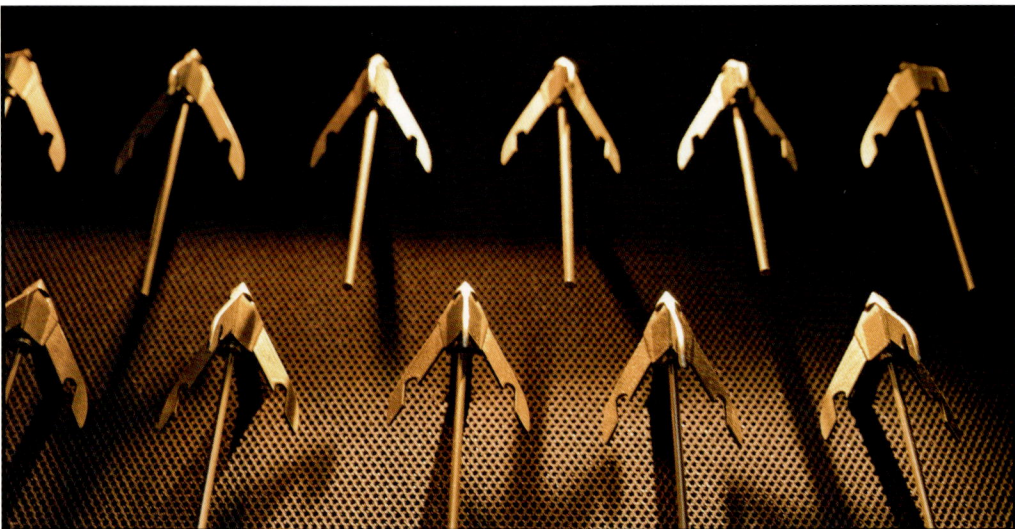

79

THE BATMOBILE RETURNS

One of the most beloved aspects of Keaton's original Batman films is the Batmobile, which was designed for both speed and combat, capable of going ninety miles per hour in five seconds. Nearly twenty feet long, its key features included side-mounted grappling hook launchers, a "foot" beneath the chassis capable of lifting and rotating the car 180 degrees, and rear oil-slick dispensers and smoke emitters.

Nico Ferrari, the picture vehicles coordinator, and Nick Murray, the picture vehicles supervisor, were honored to be entrusted with the car so it could be included in the film. As Murray comments, this version of the Batmobile has "got to be the most iconic picture car in history." Ferrari adds, "If you say to anyone, 'What's your vision of the Batmobile?' I think they instantly go to [this] one." It inspired awe in anyone who saw it on set.

A BIGGER BATWING

The Batwing needed a more significant upgrade from the original designed by Anton Furst for *Batman*. From a practical standpoint, it needed to seat more than one person. Andy Muschietti also wanted a gyroscopic rig so Batman would always remain upright in his flying position but the rest of the plane would spin around him if he were doing barrel rolls or shifting direction. Additionally, the seats needed to lower from the bottom of the Batwing, both for passengers climbing in and for when it came time to eject from the plane midflight. Dominic Tuohy and his special effects team worked tirelessly to create these features practically and make the Batwing appear fully functional. Tuohy believes that by doing these effects practically, it adds to the moment. "You can't beat physics for that," he observes. "To have actors that are actually spinning upside down, their voice changes, [as do] their positions and how they brace themselves. And when you've got Michael Keaton in the front seat being deadpan and the two boys are in the back, screaming and yelling, you can almost picture what it's gonna look like before you actually film it."

A WORLD WITHOUT SUPERMAN

In this strange new timeline, Barry quickly discovers that neither Superman nor the rest of the Justice League exist. When Bruce unearths secret military data that seems to pinpoint the hidden location of a being that matches Superman's powerset, both Barrys and Batman climb into the Batwing to journey to a missile silo, where they make an unexpected discovery.

work in progress

JOURNEY FROM THE STARS

It turns out that the being matching Superman's powerset is known as Subject Zero, a teenager named Kara Zor-El (Sasha Calle) who was sent from Krypton before it exploded to look after and protect her baby cousin Kal-El. In the original timeline, his rocket ship is found by the kindly Kents, who raise him as their own. In time Kal-El becomes the Super Hero the world knows as Superman. In this timeline, however, baby Kal-El's rocket never makes it to Earth. But Kal-El's absence isn't Kara's only shock upon arriving on Earth. Instead of being greeted with the kindness of the Kents, as moviegoers may have expected, she is captured by government agents and locked away to be studied.

SUBJECT ZERO

For two years, Kara has been imprisoned, experimented on, and tortured. Trapped in a spherical cell with Kryptonite grouting within the missile silo, far from the light of the sun, Kara has never developed the powers her cousin did in the other timeline. She experiences humanity only at its worst, represented by her captors and tormentors.

INTO THE LIGHT

Freed from her cell, Kara sees the outside world for the first time in years. The sun's rays nourish her body's cells, charging them the same way they charged Superman's. In moments, Subject Zero is gone, reborn as the mighty Supergirl, who takes flight for the first time.

Kara gains her powers without a moment to spare. The Flash's and Batman's efforts to break her out have drawn the attention of an army of mercenaries who have been guarding the missile silo. Armed with automatic weapons, they surround the heroes until Kara swoops in and defeats them one by one. Their bullets bounce off her as she uses her strength and speed to dismantle the army.

PICKING A SIDE

Kara has no reason to trust what any human has to say, including Barry. Actress Sasha Calle shares how Kara feels lost, saying, "She's hurt, and she doesn't know where she belongs. The one mission she had was to help her cousin, and he's not there." She faces an even more difficult decision upon learning that The Flash and Batman freed her to help stop General Zod and his allies, who represent the last of her people. She owes Earth nothing, but she also knows she can't let Zod go through with his genocidal plans.

A HERO'S UNIFORM

Kara's Supergirl suit shares many traits with her cousin's. Adorning her chest is her family crest, representing the House of El, which also serves as the Kryptonian symbol of hope. The symbol takes on great meaning for Kara, as Sasha Calle explains: "No matter where she's at or how hurt she is, she will always have hope, compassion, and love for all." The suit was realized for the screen by Alexandra Byrne and her talented crew of costume designers.

SUPERGIRL'S COMIC ORIGINS

When Supergirl debuted in the pages of May 1959's *Action Comics* #252, she was, fortunately, greeted by her cousin Superman. In the story by writer Otto Binder and artist Al Plastino, Supergirl explains that Argo City and its population survived Krypton's explosion. But when Argo's citizens began to succumb to Kryptonite radiation poisoning, Kara's parents, Zor-El and Alura, sent her off to Earth to be with her cousin. Hoping to get Supergirl oriented to Earth's way of life, Superman takes her to an orphanage under the name of Linda Lee while he also trains her in secret to use her powers. She soon is adopted by Fred and Edna Danvers, and in *Action Comics* #285 (February 1962), Superman formally reveals Supergirl to the world. She was welcomed with open arms.

After the events of *Flashpoint*, Supergirl has a much rockier start. In November 2011's *Supergirl* #1, by writers Michael Green and Mike Johnson and illustrator Mahmud Asrar, we see Kara crash-land in Siberia. She's consumed with confusion—first by the heavily armed men attempting to apprehend her, then by her burgeoning superpowers. Things go from bad to worse when Superman shows up. Kara last saw him as a baby on Krypton and refuses to believe this grown man wearing her family crest could be her cousin. She soon learns that while her cousin's rocket ship landed on Earth, hers was stuck in orbit around the sun for decades, leaving her in a state of suspended animation. To Kara, only days have passed since she left Krypton. All this lost time makes her acclimation to Earth even more difficult. It's clear to see how this version of Supergirl's origins influenced aspects of her appearance in *The Flash*.

ACROSS THE MULTIVERSE

Supergirl first flew into movie theaters in the summer of 1984 with the release of *Supergirl*, starring Helen Slater. The spin-off of Christopher Reeve's *Superman* film series follows Kara as she journeys to Earth in search of a powerful device known as the Omegahedron. Superman isn't present to greet her, his absence explained by a peace-seeking mission in another galaxy. However, his best pal, Jimmy Olsen (Marc McClure), makes an appearance to meet the Girl of Steel.

In 2015, *Supergirl* came to television in a series starring Melissa Benoist, which ran for six seasons. Initially set on its own unique Earth in the Multiverse, the series soon saw Supergirl meet The Flash, when Barry Allen accidentally transports himself to Supergirl's Earth and needs help getting back to his. Supergirl and The Flash later see their Earths combined in the "Crisis on Infinite Earths" crossover event on the CW network.

YOUNG FLASH, OLD SUIT

You can easily add improvisation and crafting to Barry's list of talents. As the Justice League of this new timeline is preparing for battle, the younger Barry needs a suit—in a hurry.

DRAWING INSPIRATION

Young Barry has the benefit of seeing—and wearing—his older counterpart's suit. He takes inspiration from it as he sketches his own version to wear. On paper, the design looks fully formed. But this Barry doesn't have years to develop or reproduce the silk/Teflon material of the other Barry's suit. And this timeline's Batcave has limited tools with which to work.

IF IT'S GOOD ENOUGH FOR BATMAN . . .

Batman has multiple suits left over from his crime-fighting days. He certainly isn't going to miss one of his old prototypes. While its armor isn't built to withstand the same high speeds and friction as The Flash's suit, it offers some protection for the junior speedster.

FINISHING TOUCHES

Removing the cape and adding a fresh coat of red paint makes an immediate difference. While the bat-symbol was embossed on the Batsuit, a stencil and some yellow paint do the trick for re-creating The Flash's signature lightning bolt. A pair of old headphones block out sounds and static. Kneepads and elbow pads are added for additional protection. And some yellow-and-black-striped safety tape offers just a bit of accent.

Barry works at hyper-speed to modify the boots, needing them to be more flexible and heat-resistant than the rest of the suit.

Of course, no amount of paint can cover up the suit's most signature feature—the pointy ears atop the cowl. They have to go, so Barry saws away at them with a box cutter. It is an inelegant solution, but a solution nonetheless.

THE RIGHT WAY TO RUIN A BATSUIT

Pierre Bohanna, the film's costume effects supervising modeler, had a good time developing this modified suit, which offered a unique set of creative challenges. It had to appear as a hastily made suit, but, Pierre notes "it was a lot more design than you think. . . . You can't do those things badly." The suit itself serves a means of telling the story of how the younger Barry would prepare a suit. Each level of deconstructing and altering the Batsuit needed to serve that story.

THE COMING OF ZOD

At a time when the world is unaccustomed to superpowered beings and aliens, General Zod arrives, transmitting a dire order. He accuses Earth of sheltering fellow Kryptonian Kal-El and orders the planet to turn him over within twenty-four hours or suffer great consequences.

GENERAL ZOD

In the film *Man of Steel*, General Zod, the leader of Krypton's Warrior Guild, leads a coup to overthrow the Kryptonian Council. He believes Krypton's leaders have brought the planet to the brink of ruin and that only he can restore it. Both righteous and ruthless, Zod is willing to kill anyone who stands in his way.

Zod's plot includes creating a master race of Kryptonians by removing what he deems are "degenerative bloodlines." To accomplish his mission, he needs an ancient artifact known as the Codex, which contains all Kryptonian genetic information and is used to produce new life through artificial reproduction. (Natural birth has been outlawed for centuries.) Needing to hide the Codex in a place Zod could never reach, Jor-El encodes it within the DNA of his son, Kal-El, before rocketing him off to Earth.

Zod's insurgency is ultimately foiled. He and his soldiers—known as the Sword of Rao—are sentenced to the Phantom Zone, an interdimensional prison, which inadvertently leads to their salvation because they're off-planet when Krypton explodes. When they emerge from the Phantom Zone decades later, Zod resumes his search for Kal-El and the Codex.

FAORA-UL

Zod's subcommander, Faora-Ul (Antje Traue), is cold and calculating. She is fully committed to Zod's cause, fighting with precision and an unflinching, ice-cold demeanor. Free of any sense of mercy or regret, Faora fights to win at any cost. Traue describes Faora by saying, "Violence is her satisfaction.... I thought there should be no subtext, no double meaning for her. This is what she is. She's trained to attack good men, just to protect her Krypton."

NAM-EK

Over nine feet tall, this towering giant is genetically engineered to be the ideal soldier. He is obedient and relentless, carrying out any order demanded of him. Already imposing thanks to his size, Nam-Ek is an absolutely terrifying force when he wears his full armor.

THE WORLD ENGINE

As depicted in *Man of Steel*, retrieving the Codex is just the first stage of Zod's plan. From his ship, *Black Zero*, he plans to use a device known as the World Engine to terraform Earth and alter its atmosphere to be more hospitable to Kryptonian life-forms. Humankind will be eradicated in the process. In the original timeline, Superman is able to stop the World Engine and destroy *Black Zero* with the help of Lois Lane (Amy Adams), scientist Emil Hamilton (Richard Schiff), and air force colonel Nathan Hardy (Christopher Meloni). But in a world without Superman, humanity faces extinction at Zod's hands.

DARK FLASH

The specter of Dark Flash lurks throughout the film The Flash, an unknown threat that will show itself when the moment is right. Dark Flash is Barry's opposite, someone who refuses to accept loss and move on. The long-term effect of using the Speed Force to manipulate time has warped Dark Flash's mind. He can no longer be reasoned with, and his obsessive drive has made him even more powerful than Barry. Producer Barbara Muschietti adds that Dark Flash is willing to achieve his mission at the "cost of every timeline."

DEATH FOR SPEEDSTERS

The look of Dark Flash recalls the Black Flash, who first appeared in *The Flash* #138 (June 1998). In the comics, the Black Flash represents one of the darkest aspects of the Speed Force. It's an entity that acts as Grim Reaper to speedsters and appears whenever it's a speedster's time to become one with the Speed Force. It also seeks to reclaim anyone who has entered the Speed Force and later escaped.

THE JUSTICE LEAGUE REBORN

They're a far cry from the Justice League that defeated Steppenwolf, but they're all that's standing between Zod and the survival of the planet.

LEARNING FROM PAST MISTAKES

When the fight against Zod starts to go south, and both Batman's and Supergirl's lives are in danger, Young Barry decides he, too, must manipulate time to save his new friends. Despite being aware of the changes to reality that his older self caused, Young Barry ventures into the Chronobowl with hopes of changing the course of the fight. He'll soon discover that his actions place the fate of two realities in jeopardy.

THE FINISH LINE

After the battle against Zod, Barry faces a difficult decision. He's seen firsthand just how delicate the space-time continuum is. Can he let go of the past and restore the present to what it once was? Can the present even be restored? Or is the damage already done? Only time will tell. Fortunately, Barry has time on his side.

Published by Titan Books, London, in 2023.

TITAN BOOKS

A division of Titan Publishing Group Ltd
144 Southwark Street
London SE1 0UP
www.titanbooks.com

Find us on Facebook: www.facebook.com/TitanBooks
Follow us on Twitter: @titanbooks

Copyright © 2023 DC & Warner Bros. Entertainment Inc. THE FLASH and all related characters and elements © & ™ DC and Warner Bros. Entertainment Inc. WB SHIELD: © & ™ WBEI. (s23)

Batman created by Bob Kane with Bill Finger.

Supergirl based on characters created by Jerry Siegel and Joe Shuster. By special arrangement with the Jerry Siegel family.

Published by arrangement with Insight Editions, San Rafael, California.
www.insighteditions.com

No part of this publication may be reproduced, stored in a retrieval system, or transmitted, in any form or by any means without the prior written permission of the publisher, nor be otherwise circulated in any form of binding or cover other than that in which it is published and without a similar condition being imposed on the subsequent purchaser.

A CIP catalogue record for this title is available from the British Library.

ISBN: 9781803365992

Publisher: Raoul Goff
VP, Co-Publisher: Vanessa Lopez
VP, Creative: Chrissy Kwasnik
VP, Manufacturing: Alix Nicholaeff
VP, Group Managing Editor: Vicki Jaeger
Publishing Director: Jamie Thompson
Designer: Brooke McCullum
Editor: Anna Wostenberg
Editorial Assistant: Sami Alvarado
Managing Editor: Maria Spano
Senior Production Editor: Katie Rokakis
Senior Production Manager: Greg Steffen
Senior Production Manager, Subsidiary Rights: Lina s Palma-Temena

Insight Editions, in association with Roots of Peace, will plant two trees for each tree used in the manufacturing of this book. Roots of Peace is an internationally renowned humanitarian organization dedicated to eradicating land mines worldwide and converting war-torn lands into productive farms and wildlife habitats. Roots of Peace will plant two million fruit and nut trees in Afghanistan and provide farmers there with the skills and support necessary for sustainable land use.

Manufactured in China by Insight Editions

10 9 8 7 6 5 4 3 2 1